THIS OLD STORE

By

Aaron McAlexander

ISBN-13 978-0-9854225-2-3

Printed in U.S.A.

CONTENTS

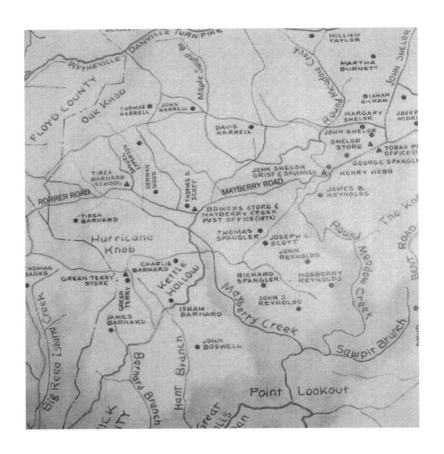

Mayberry, Virginia, about 1870.
(Courtesy of Annalee Shelor.)

Introduction

Life has never been very easy in Mayberry. From the time it was first settled, most of the people here have made their living from the ground, working small hilly farms and getting by with whatever they could grow or build for themselves. The soil here is fertile, but most of the fields are steep and hard to till, and the first farmers who settled here had to clear the timber from the land before they could even begin to grow crops. The isolation of the community made it hard to market whatever surplus the farms might have produced, and for many years, it was hard for the folks in Mayberry to obtain the few essential things that they could not make or grow for themselves and needed to buy.

This part of the Blue Ridge Mountains was settled somewhat later than most of southwest Virginia. The Great Wagon Road that so many of the early settlers followed southward out of Pennsylvania and into Virginia and the Carolinas split into two branches at the southern end of the Shenandoah Valley. The eastern branch, called the *Carolina Road*, meandered southward through the Piedmont, while the western branch, called the *Frontier Trail*, passed far to the north and west of this part of the Blue Ridge. The Carolina Road formed the connections that led to piedmont towns such as Martinsville and Greensboro, and the Frontier Trail led to the settlement of mountain towns such as Wytheville and Abington. The area where the Virginia counties of Carroll, Floyd, and Patrick Counties come together was largely bypassed. Most of the early settlers in Mayberry moved here after having first lived in nearby Virginia counties such as Pittsylvania or Floyd, or in the North Carolina counties of Surry or Stokes. Some of the communities in that area continue to be somewhat isolated, and one of them, of course, is *Mayberry*.

For the first hundred years of Mayberry's existence, its denizens had to work from dawn to dusk just to stay alive. The plantation economy that once existed in much of the South had little relevance to the people living in these Appalachian Mountains. Even by 1900, the typical Mayberry family probably wouldn't have seen fifty dollars of cash money in a year's time; selling a hog or a calf for five dollars or a bushel of chestnuts for fifty cents was considered a windfall. References are often made to the *family farm* when describing Mayberry, and that's because it really was an enterprise which required the involvement of the entire family. A farmer needed a lot of help to make a living from this mountainous land, so the children began working on the farm from a very young age. When the mother wasn't busy having more kids, she was usually in the field, helping with the farm work as well.

Sometimes you might have heard some of the farm folks up here talk about how lucky they were to be living in these mountains, where they didn't have to prime tobacco and they didn't have to chop cotton. That was true, so far as it went, since neither cotton nor burley tobacco will grow at the nearly 3000 foot elevation of Mayberry. But it is also true that there were no crops that could be grown here that would bring in as much money as could be made from cotton or tobacco. The staple crops of this region were corn and buckwheat, which, grown on sloping fields and without the benefit of fertilizer, often produced sparse yields. These mountain folks so valued their independence, however, that it was viewed as a sad occasion whenever a family found it necessary to give up working their mountain farm in exchange for a life of labor inside of the cotton mills in Danville or the furniture factories in Bassett. Many of the people who had to make that move came right back to these mountains as soon as they were able.

Probably the most profitable crop ever grown around Mayberry was corn, especially after it had been transformed into a liquid form for more efficient transportation. But that kind of commerce was not for everyone. Many of the citizens of Mayberry had strong religious objections to any and all commerce involving liquid corn products, but that would be the subject of another story.

In the early times, if someone decided to seek their fortune in Mayberry, there were but a few options. To be successful in farming, one needed sufficient land and a large family. Although hunting and fishing once were an important part of providing food for a family, game had become scarce by the twentieth century. Many men were able to supplement their livelihood with self-taught skills such as carpentry and blacksmithing, but there were fewer options for the women. A woman's role was mostly limited to housekeeping and helping out on the farm, and for a few of them, either nursing or teaching school.

There were periodic booms in timber cutting and saw milling around Mayberry before and after the turn of the twentieth century, but the pay was poor, especially considering that it was such hard and dangerous work. During this same period, many young men from the area decided to take their chances by working in the mines of West Virginia, where the dangers were also considerable, but the pay was much better. Like many international immigrants of today, those who went to work in the mines would often send whatever money they could back to their families in Mayberry. Some learned useful skills from their work in the mines, often bringing them back and applying them here.

There are a lot of swift creeks and streams in these mountains. With a little knowledge and a lot of hard work, a man could possibly have dammed up a mountain stream and built a water powered grist mill or a sawmill. Several local entrepreneurs did just that, some with amazing results. Ed Mabry's now famous *Mabry Mill,* just four miles to the north of Mayberry via the Blue Ridge Parkway, is one of the few survivors of many such endeavors.

With a little capital and a good sense of value, perhaps a man could have become a merchant and operated a general store. There should have been significant opportunity in providing the material needs of these hardy mountain folk that they could not produce for themselves. That opportunity prompted the business decision made by the Scott brothers, Simon Peter, Samuel Cephas, and James Rufus.

The Mayberry Store

The Name

Which came first, the community called Mayberry, or the Mayberry Store? This is a question often asked by visitors when they come into *The Mayberry Trading Post,* and while the question is simple enough, it is not all that easy to give a simple answer. Some might say that the year the community of Mayberry became official was 1895, the year that the government changed the name of the post office from *Mayberry Creek* to just plain **Mayberry**. Actually though, the folks around here had been calling this community *Mayberry* for years before that change occurred. And just to confuse the matter, there are documents that date back to long before the Civil War that make reference to this area, but using the name *Mabry Creek*.

While this old store has had several different names, some of the folks who were around back in the eighteen eighties said that it was always called "The Mayberry Store," no matter who was running it. But none of those real "old-timers" could seem to recall whether the original store had a sign on the front indicating its name. My grandma thought that the customers who did their trading at the Mayberry Store lived so close by that a sign was probably unnecessary.

It is clear, however, that the name of both the Old *Mayberry* Store and that of the surrounding community of *Mayberry*, Virginia, came from the last name of some of the early settlers in this part of the country. If you have traveled on the Southern Virginia section of the Blue Ridge Parkway, then you surely must have noticed *Mabry Mill*, the scenic old water-powered mill situated right beside the Parkway near milepost 176. That mill was built in the early 1900's by Edward Boston Mabry, a fifth generation descendant of some folks of that same last name who lived near here. Both Mayberry and Mabry are surnames that were once common in this area and that have a common origin.

The name that became the name of this *Mayberry* probably originated in North America in 1679, when Frances *Maybury*, of Sussex County, England, came to Henrico County, Virginia. (There were also some *Mayberrys* who came to Pennsylvania from Germany somewhat later, but they do not seem to have been connected to the Mayberrys of Mayberry.) The progeny of Frances Maybury became widely scattered throughout the southeastern part of the country, with some of the descendants adopting the name *Mabry* and some others spelling their last name as *Mayberry*. These different forms of the name are to be expected, given that many of these early settlers could not read and write, and some of those who could may not have been good spellers.

A descendant of Frances Maybury, Isaac Mabry, obtained a grant for 183 acres of land on the "south side of Robertson's Creek" in 1792. The name of that same creek was later changed to *Mayberry Creek* in honor of Isaac Mabry. The Mayberry Trading Post is only about a quarter of a mile from that stream, which has now been known as *Mayberry Creek* for about a century and a half.

The Patrick County, Virginia, Tax records from the early 1800's list persons with the last names of Scott, Spangler, and Wood as having paid taxes on land described as being located "on the waters of Mabry Creek." By the 1870's, however, the location of land in the same area was being described in the tax records as being located near "Mayberry Creek."

The first business of record in the area now called Mayberry was the *Hefflefinger Mill*, which was constructed on Mayberry Creek sometime in the 1850's. Henry and Angelina Hefflefinger sold their mill to Joseph G. Scott in 1888, and it was continuously in operation, run by Joseph Scott and others, until well into the 1900's.

The earliest reference to a store in Mayberry mentions the "storehouse" begun by William Bower in 1858. The storehouse was described as being near Mayberry Creek and located at the intersection of the two roads known then as the *Wildcat Road* and *Rorrer Road*. The names of the roads that run along approximately those same routes today are respectively known as *Mayberry Church Road* and *Hurricane Ridge Road*. The current *Mayberry Trading Post* is located at that same intersection.

The junction of those two well-traveled roads was a logical place to build a store (or a storehouse), even a hundred and fifty years ago. The store was built facing the *Wildcat Road*, a road that connected with the *Bellspur Road* and wound down the mountain and (eventually) to Mt. Airy, North Carolina, the nearest town with access to a railroad.

There are a few folks around who can still recall just how that old first store building looked. Until the nineteen twenties, it continued to stand right beside the building that is now the Mayberry Trading Post. And while it is true that the old store in Mayberry has had several different *official* names during its many years of operation, then as well as now, when someone simply made a reference to *The Mayberry Store*, anyone from the area would have known exactly the place that they were referring to.

The Scotts

Thomas and Lucinda Scott raised their seven children in a house that stood not far behind the current location of the Mayberry Trading Post, and the sons in that Scott family provided much of the driving force that created the viable community that once was Mayberry. At a time when the area was populated almost entirely by subsistence farmers, some of the Scott boys built and operated several businesses. The enterprises established by Simon Peter (b.1857), Samuel Cephas (b.1863), James Rufus (b.1870), and their cousin Joseph G. Scott significantly improved the local economy and helped to create a better quality of life for the people of this isolated mountain community.

In 1872, after Simon Scott married Mollie Bower, the daughter of store owner William Bower, Simon began helping his father-in-law with the Mayberry Store. He was the first one of the Scott Brother's to enter into the store business, but when William Bower decided to return to his old home near Floyd, Virginia, it was Simon's brother

Cephas who bought out Bower's interest in the store and joined his brother in running the store.

Because two of the Scott brothers were sometimes known by multiple names, there is always the possibility of confusion regarding the men who were associated with the Mayberry store. *Simon Peter Scott,* for example, was sometimes known by his full Biblical name, "Simon Peter," but in Mayberry, he was usually just known as Simon. Later in life, however, he was sometimes known as "Simon the Tanner," to distinguish him from a Simon Scott of another generation,

Samuel Cephas Scott was usually known as S.C. Scott by the people with whom he conducted business, and the Mayberry Store was officially known as *S.C. Scott's Store* for a number of years. Local folk and acquaintances would sometimes call him *Cephas,* but most often, he was simply known as *Ceph.* Apparently, no one ever called him by his first name, Samuel.

James Rufus Scott was considered the fortunate son in the name department of that family, since everyone in Mayberry always just called him *Jim.*

The Simon Peter Scott house, built around 1905.

The Post Office

It is also not so easy to give a simple answer to the simple question, "How long has Mayberry been in existence?" One logical response might be "since 1872," the year that the *Mayberry Creek Post Office* first began its operation. The first "Mayberry Creek Post Office" was located in the home of Jehu Barnard, its first postmaster. That placed the post office at the foot of Hurricane Knob and right beside Rorrer Road, about a half mile to the west of the Mayberry Store. When Simon Scott became post master in 1883, however, he was able to get the Mayberry Creek Post

Office moved into the Mayberry Store, a central location which was more convenient both for him and for many other Mayberry residents.

The Scott Brothers soon expanded the operation of their store to include a *mercantile exchange*, a business that bought livestock, poultry, and produce from the local farmers and delivered these farm products to stockyards and wholesalers in the nearest towns. In the early days, most of the local goods bought by the Mayberry store were resold in Mount Airy, North Carolina, the nearest town with a railway connection. After the Danville and Western Railway came to Stuart, Virginia in 1891, however, the Mayberry Store began a lively trade with businesses located in Stuart.

In the early 1890's, the business became so prosperous that a third Scott Brother, James, was taken in as a partner, and the enterprise became officially known as *Scott Brother's Store*. The business soon outgrew the little original structure, so construction on a new and larger building was begun. The new store was located right beside the old one, just a few yards to the north. If there was a grand opening celebration when the new store building opened, there is no record of it to be found.

Years ago, longtime Mayberry resident and former mail carrier, J.H. (Dump) Yeatts (1870-1967) told the author that his recollection of the sign which was originally placed on the tall false front of the newly completed store building was one which simply labeled it as *Mayberry Store*. He also recalled how the old original store building remained there beside the "new" store for many years, functioning as a feed, fertilizer, and farm implement storage building. (The "new" fertilizer shed that replaced the old original storehouse in the 1930's is the small building still standing about thirty yards to the north of the Mayberry Trading Post.)

As is so often the case, the three partners in the Mayberry Store did not always agree on the business model that should be followed, and the coalition of Scott Brothers eventually was dissolved. Simon Scott, who also worked as a shoe maker, harness maker, and carpenter, decided to leave the store to go into the tanning and leather goods business. He built himself a shoe and harness shop beside Rorrer Road, about a quarter of a mile to the west of the store and he later built a tannery on the hillside across from his leather shop. James Scott bought a lumber mill and abandoned the store business just a few years later, leaving S.C. Scott as sole owner of the Mayberry Store.

When S.C. Scott became the postmaster in 1895, he was able to get the name of the post office officially changed to *Mayberry Post Office.* Soon after that, the name *S. C. Scott's Store,* was painted onto the high false front of the store in large bold letters, and below the name of the store, in a bold but smaller notation, *U. S. Post Office, Mayberry, Va.* was painted across the front. The area behind the counter in the back right hand corner of the store became the post office for *Mayberry, Virginia,* complete with post office boxes, a postmark and cancellation stamp, a safe, and even a green eyeshade; everything that any official United States Post Office should have.

Back then, government jobs were even more politically connected than they are today, and the position of postmaster had an even higher rate of turnover than most.. S. C. Scott managed to hang on to his job longer than most, keeping his postmaster's job for over fourteen years before being replaced by Charlie Harrell in 1910. Charlie Harrell was able to serve as postmaster for just four years before being replaced by William Boyd. And William Boyd served as postmaster for just five years before S.C. Scott regained the position in 1919. S.C. Scott was both the first and the last postmaster at the *Mayberry Post Office*, his job as postmaster ending when the government closed the post office in 1922.

The Mayberry Post Office suffered the fate of many other small post offices in the nineteen twenties, as an increase in the use of automobiles and an improvement of the roads extended the reach of individual mail carriers and made the operation of so many small, rural post offices uneconomical. When the United States Post Office in Mayberry, Virginia, was shuttered in 1922, the Mayberry postal route was taken over by the larger post office in Meadows of Dan. When J.H. Yeatts, who had been the Mayberry mail carrier for many years, began delivering the mail to Mayberry residents out of the larger post office at *Meadows of Dan*, the postal address "Mayberry, Virginia," ceased to exist. The community surrounding the Mayberry Store, however, continued to be known as Mayberry and it is still known by that name today. Although the name *Mayberry* disappeared from the listing of the U.S. Post Offices over ninety years ago, the community of Mayberry is still very much alive in the hearts of a lot of people, myself included, who have a very strong attachment to this part of the Blue Ridge Mountains.

The people who have operated the store, from S.C. Scott on down, have carefully maintained the names that were posted on the old "pigeon hole" post office boxes in the back of the store at the time the post office was closed. Those names are a roll call of the long departed residents of Mayberry, folks who once lived within walking distance of the Mayberry Post Office. The names, in the order they appeared on the boxes, are:

S. P. Scott	Jim Turman
John Barnard	Lum Stanley
Jasper Hensley	Mack McCormick
Jack Childress	R.H.B. Terry
Dewey Stanley	Grover Marshall
J.E. Wood	John Kimble
Richard Marshall	Jim Chandler
Kirby Banks	Tilden Banks
Fred Banks	Jim Banks
Lee Smith	George Terry

The fee for keeping an official P.O. Box was about 50 cents per year back then, but for some, that was still too much. Others were unwilling to put up a roadside mail box. The Mayberry postmasters were not required to do so, but they just kept the mail for those folks tucked safely under the counter until they could come by and pick it up.

The Times, They Do Change

Not long after the post office was shut down, Ceph Scott's health began to fail, and he just seemed to lose a lot of his interest in the store. Harried by debt and domestic discord, Ceph left his wife and family. While they continued to live in the fine Edwardian home beside Mayberry Road that he had built for them twenty years earlier, Ceph began living in makeshift quarters in the back of the Mayberry Store. The little back room of the store is where he was sleeping on the night he passed away in August of 1926.

The business had been in a state of decline for some years before Ceph Scott passed away, and the last straw came with the depression. The store was soon closed down and it remained closed until it was bought by J.H. Yeatts and his son Coy in 1934. The store building required a great deal of repair before it was reopened by the Yeatts brothers, Coy and Hassell, and when it finally did reopen, the name had been changed to *Yeatts Brothers' Store*. The younger Yeatts brother, Hassell, participated in the operation of the store for only a few months, however, before he decided that he was not cut out for the life of a store keeper and withdrew from the partnership. The name *Yeatts Brothers Store* was retained on the high false front, however, until 1969, when the store was renamed the *Mayberry Trading Post*.

Going back as far as the history of the store can be documented, the following are the names under which the store operated and the names of the proprietors.

YEARS	NAME OF STORE	PROPRIETOR
1872 – 1892	Mayberry Store	Scott brothers
1892 – 1926	S.C. Scott's Store	S.C. Scott
1934 – 1969	Yeatts Brothers' Store	Coy O. Yeatts
1969 – 1984	Mayberry Trading Post	Addie Wood
1984 – 2005	" "	Coy Lee and Dale Yeatts
2006 – 2012	" "	Dale Yeatts
2012 –	Mayberry Trading Post	Peggy Barkley

To appreciate the Mayberry Store as it must have been a hundred years ago, it is helpful to understand how much the environment and the community around Mayberry have changed in the century past. To begin looking into the past, one might stand in front of the old store building and look up Mayberry Church Road to the north and then look down the road to the south. Look directly across the road from the store, and then walk around the store and look to the west, across the Blue Ridge Parkway. Finally, imagine that all of the surrounding land that you can see is completely cleared of trees.

Mayberry was mostly a farming community from its earliest beginnings, but the second largest economic activity was timber cutting and saw milling. The woodlands which cover so much of this area of the Blue Ridge Mountains today are of second and third growth reforestation. Most of the land in Mayberry that could be farmed was cleared by the beginning of the twentieth century. The woodlands that surround the Mayberry of today are relatively young, having filled in many open fields in the time that has passed since the Second World War.

Woods were sometimes allowed to take over the fields simply because of the poor farming practices that had allowed the fertile topsoil to be eroded away. Folks can still remember when there were barren and gullied fields on hills all around Mayberry. Some of the ruined fields were even given descriptive names such as Gully Hill or Ace's Old New Ground. Unfortunately, some of the old farming practices, such as not rotating crops or failing to plant cover crops and leaving the fields exposed throughout the winter are not entirely a thing of the past.

It may be hard to imagine, but until about 1970, the road in front of the Mayberry Store was even narrower than it is now. The edge of the road was about six feet farther from the front of the store and the road bed was a couple of feet lower. Back then, there was plenty of room to park in front of the store or to pull up to the gas pump for fueling. And, in case you are wondering, there has been a "loafers bench" (some called it a "liar's bench") sitting on posts in front of the store for as far back as anyone can remember.

If you go into the Mayberry Trading Post today, it might strike you as being kind of dark inside. Actually though, it is pretty bright compared to how dark it was in there before electricity came to Mayberry in 1949. Consider how the windows on either side of the store's front door are almost as tall as the room itself. The tall windows were put there to admit as much light as was practicable, since both sides of the store were completely covered up with shelves. Those two windows, supplemented by a kerosene lamp or two, provided all of the lighting in the store whenever the front doors were closed. In the summer, when the double front doors were sometimes left open, the open doors nearly doubled the illumination of the interior of the store. Before electrification, light in the interior of the store must really have been minimal on cloudy winter days, and the lack of lighting is probably why the Mayberry Store usually closed about five o'clock.

Surprisingly, the folks operating store did not have to wait for electricity to come to Mayberry before they had access to refrigeration, of sorts. In the earliest days, some perishable items, such as butter and produce were kept in a spring house that stood near the store. But when Coy Yeatts began running the store, one of the first improvements he made was the introduction of a kerosene powered refrigerator. (That may seem strange, but kerosene and propane powered refrigerators are still available. They continue to be manufactured for people in remote areas that do not have electricity and for groups such as the Amish, who by choice, do not use electricity.)

Probably, the most significant difference in the land surrounding the store was that there was no Blue Ridge Parkway cleaving through Mayberry before 1937. The land behind the store was mostly open fields, many of them surrounded by chestnut rail fences and interspersed with houses, barns, and sheds. All three of the Scott Brothers associated with the Mayberry store, Simon, Cephas, and Jim, lived within a half mile of the store. Their mother, Lucinda Scott, lived in a house on the little knoll behind the store until her death in 1928. The fine Edwardian home built by Simon Scott still stands beside Hurricane Ridge Road, less than a quarter of a mile to the west of the store. A house of similar stature was built by Cephas Scott about 1905. That house, which functioned as a bed and breakfast until just a few years ago, still stands right beside Mayberry Church Road, about a half mile to the north.

The Old Store is really showing its age these days, but there is much more to the story of the Mayberry Store than the history of the old building. The real story of the store is the history of the hardworking people who have kept this icon of the mountain community going all these years, through good times and bad, and about the good people of Mayberry, mostly now departed, for whom it was the center of their community. A big part of the story of the store today is about the travelers from the Parkway who take the time to stop and visit. There are many visitors who stop by to take pictures of the store, but who also show an interest in the history of the old store and the story of original Mayberry. These are the kind of people who appreciate a historical treasure when they find one.

In the rural America of a simpler time, there were three institutions that determined the identity of any small community. They were the community's church, its school, and the general store. Today, the Mayberry Presbyterian church is thriving, but the school is long gone. And as for the store, whether it is called the *Mayberry Trading Post*, the *Mayberry Store*, *Yeatts' Store*, or *S.C. Scott's Store*, the continued existence of the community of Mayberry itself may be dependent upon the continued existence of the store.

Old photograph showing both the Bower Storehouse and the S.C. Scott Store.
Photograph attributed to Mrs. Ella Scott, circa 1895.
(Courtesy of Tony Woods.)

S.C. Scott's Store

Construction began on the "new" Mayberry Store building in 1892. The Scott brothers hired Wallace Spangler to build the store, and Simon and James Scott both helped with the construction. For several years before that, the Scott brothers operated the Mayberry Store out of the small building just south of the store's present location. After the new store building was completed, the old store building remained and was used as a storage shed for feed, fertilizer, hardware, and farm implements until almost 1930.

The partnership between S.C. Scott and his brothers was dissolved sometime before the turn of the century and S.C. Scott, known to most of his customers as "Ceph," became the sole proprietor of the store.

The first of the Scott brothers to have an interest in the Mayberry Store was Simon, a man of many practical skills. He was a carpenter, a cobbler, a tanner, a saddle and harness maker, and a brick mason who made his own bricks. Sometime in the 1890's, Simon decided to put those skills to work and create a business all his own, so he sold his partnership in the store to his brothers and began concentrating on his leather business. Simon Scott first built a shop beside Rorrer Road in which he made and sold shoes, saddles, and harnesses. Then he began construction on a tannery, not simply to supply the raw material for his own leather business, but he also because he planned to tan and sell hides for businesses in Stuart and Mt. Airy.

The two-story brick structure Simon Scott built for his tannery was the most imposing building that had ever been constructed in Mayberry at the time. The tannery was Simon's own design and it was built over large tanning vats that were dug into the ground and lined with tongue and grooved chestnut boards. Simon Scott did most of the carpentry and brickwork himself, even making his own bricks. (He also made the bricks used to build the support pillars underneath the Trading Post building and for the foundation of the house he built on Hurricane Ridge Road.)

Simon's old tannery building was constructed on the hillside to the right of Rorrer Road (now Hurricane Ridge Road), about 0.2 miles to the west of the Mayberry Trading Post. Although he gave up the tanning business in the 1930's, the tannery building remained in place until about 1970. There is currently a horse barn that is approximately the size as the old tannery building standing in precisely the same location where the tannery once stood.

Simon Scott was not a maker of fine dress shoes, but he concentrated instead on the practical and sturdy work shoes and brogans that most of the people of Mayberry wore for everyday use. He could make custom-fitted shoes if the customer required them, but he mostly made more-or-less standard sized shoes and boots that he sold from his shop and through the Mayberry Store.

Although Simon the Tanner lived until 1944, the times in Mayberry were changing long before then, and he gave up his shoe making and tanning business in the 1930's. Although, for the rest of his life, he would occasionally be called upon to mend a pair of shoes or a fix a harness, the transition from the horse to the automobile had made most of Simon Scott's exceptional skills obsolete.

Simon Peter Scott and Volney Reynolds at Simon's tannery, circa 1925. (Photo courtesy of Alberta and Lawrence Sewell.)

There are no records to be found that describe all of the merchandise stocked in the Scott Store circa 1900, but through the memories of my grandparents and my uncles and aunts, I learned a few things about the merchandise carried there over the years. My uncles and aunts, all born and raised in Mayberry in the early 1900's, used to reminisce about their trips to S.C. Scott's store when they were children, and they would talk about some of the things they would buy there. They recalled that the Scott store mostly stocked essentials, common items that everyone needed but most people could not make for themselves. For some folks, that was a surprisingly small number of items, but there were always a few of the basics that everyone had to buy.

For feeding the family, there were things such as salt, sugar, coffee and flour that came from the store, not to mention the pots and pans that the food was cooked in. If it was a bad year for crops, large bags of dried pinto beans and slabs of pork belly might be added to the list of essential purchases. In really bad years, S.C. Scott often carried the tab for folks who could not pay until times got better.

Periodically, the store would get a shipment of salt fish, usually either herring or cod, preserved in a strong solution of brine and tightly packed into large wooden barrels. Salt fish was a staple of rural general stores all over the country throughout the nineteenth century and well into the twentieth. Even I can remember when a barrel of salt herring was usually sitting right in front of the counter in a general store. When someone wanted to buy some salt fish, the clerk would "fish" them right out of the barrel of brine with a large fork and plop them down, still dripping, on a piece of brown paper laid out on the top of the counter. Before those salt fish were cooked, however, they had to be soaked in fresh water for at least a day and preferably for two. Without a thorough pre-soaking, salt preserved fish are just too darn salty for human consumption.

In the clothing department, there were the leather work boots, the rubber arctics and galoshes, the denim overalls and jackets, and the heavy work gloves that were an important part of the Mayberry Store's stock maintained for the community of farmers.

Even the most independent farmer would have to occasionally buy farm tools from the store: corn huskers, corn cutters, hoes, pitch forks, knives and whet stones, sheep shears, oil lamps and lanterns, horse shoes and horse collars. Then there was always the need for basic hardware items, so nails, screws, bolts, and hinges must have been a part of the regular stock at the store. And whether for sport or for food, there was always the need for fish hooks and shotgun shells.

There were a few "luxury" items to be found in the store as well. For the kids who would occasionally come in with a penny or two to spend, the store was stocked with plenty of candy. There were many adults in Mayberry who appreciated having the luxury of snuff, chewing tobacco, and smoking tobacco available, all in a variety of brands. Packs of ready rolled cigarettes may also have been in stock, but most cigarette smokers back then bought little bags or tins of cut tobacco and cigarette papers so they could "roll-their-own." Although S.C. Scott was not licensed to sell any alcoholic beverages in his store, he did carry a large inventory of patent medicines, and there were a few savvy customers who knew which of the cure-alls contained high percentages of alcohol. But if Dr. Baker's Blood Builder was not one's cup of tea, both the lemon and the almond extracts sold in the store checked out at about eighty proof.

One essential commodity that surely was available at the Mayberry Store, probably from the day the store opened, was "lamp oil." Until a few years after the Civil War, most of the families in Mayberry had been using home-made tallow candles for lighting. Even if the "coal oil" and the lamps in which it was used had been available, they would have been too expensive for a lot of folks. With the introduction of relatively inexpensive kerosene as a replacement for coal oil, however, the use of oil lamps became more affordable. My grandmother recalled buying a "pretty nice" kerosene lamp at the Scott Store for 25¢, and she was delighted when she saw that the light from the oil lamp outshone the light from a candle many times over.

The kerosene oil lamp had a profound impact on life in places like Mayberry around the turn of the twentieth century. With the increasing availability of kerosene lamps and lanterns, people were no longer dependent on daylight for working, reading, and traveling. It is difficult to exaggerate the importance of lamps and lamp oil in a community that did not have electric power. The Mayberry Store has kept kerosene lamps in stock from its very beginning until today. Those kerosene lamps still come in handy when the power goes off, whether you are in Mayberry or someplace else.

Kerosene was often referred to as "lamp oil" until more recent times, when folks started using it in kerosene space heaters, but kerosene has always had a lot of important uses in addition to fuel for lamps and stoves. Kerosene is hard to beat for quickly starting a wood fire, early Fordson tractors ran on kerosene, and it used to be about the only thing anyone in Mayberry ever used to clean out a paint brush. I even knew a fellow folks who would put a little kerosene on a rag and tie it around his neck whenever he felt a sore throat coming on.

There was a square, steel kerosene tank that sat just inside the door of the addition on the north side of the store for many years,. The "lamp oil" was dispensed by a hand cranked pump mounted on the top of the tank, a gallon or two at a time. When customers would come in with their metal kerosene cans, the clerk dispensing the kerosene would first crank the pump handle in one direction, causing a rod in the base of the pump to rise up from the tank. The handle was then cranked in the opposite direction until the rod returned all of the way into the tank, indicating that one gallon of lamp oil had been pumped. I think that method of dispensing kerosene has varied little over the many years that the Mayberry Store has existed.

Some of the men of Mayberry went away to work in the coal mines of West Virginia and returned bringing a new lighting technology with them. The head lamps they had been using in the mines were the new lightweight and reliable acetylene lamps, fueled by a gas created when water is added to bits of calcium carbide. Carbide lamps and lanterns were somewhat more expensive and messy than their kerosene equivalents, but they gave off a brighter light and burned longer without refueling. Carbide lanterns were the standard technology for headlamps on buggies and early automobiles for many years, and carbide lighting systems were even used in homes for a while.

Sometime around 1920, a smooth-talking traveling salesman convinced Simon Scott, J.H. Yeatts, and some other Mayberry residents that they should install modern acetylene lighting systems in their homes. The acetylene systems that he sold them worked pretty well for a couple of years, but eventually they became hopelessly clogged and useless. The quick lime residue produced by the carbide gas generators, however, provided enough material to whitewash every chicken house in Mayberry for years after the home lighting systems had stopped working. And for many years, the Mayberry Store was well stocked with canisters of calcium carbide for anyone who still happened to use acetylene lamps.

The original lamp oil dispenser from S.C. Scott's store, used around 1900. (Courtesy of L.H.Hutchens.)

Over the years, the Scott Store became much more than a business where the Mayberry folks would just visit to purchase their essential "store-bought" goods. In the early years of the twentieth century, the store began effectively functioning as an agricultural exchange or brokerage. The local farmers either sold their products for cash or they traded them to the store for the goods they needed. The products that local farmers most often exchanged at the store included butter, eggs, cabbage, potatoes, turnips, apples (both fresh and dried), nuts, berries, and wool. S.C. Scott's Store really was a "trading post," back then.

The Scott Store did a lot of dealing in livestock and poultry also. The store bought and sold different kinds of locally raised animals, including sheep, hogs, and cattle, and a variety of fowl, including chickens, geese, Guinea fowl, and turkeys. Ceph Scott kept stock pens and poultry houses behind the store building and on land he owned across Mayberry Road from the store. (When a parcel of land near the store recently changed hands, the deed was found to still contain a caveat giving S.C. Scott perpetual access to his chicken houses. That restriction had been in the deed since Mr. Scott sold the land in 1923.)

Of all of the local products purchased by S.C. Scott and shipped out of Mayberry, the one most important to the largest number of people was definitely the American Chestnut. From the time when these mountains were inhabited by Native Americans and early European settlers until the nineteen twenties, the native chestnut was truly a bounty provided by nature. Until the demise of the chestnut, many Mayberry families were dependent on the fall chestnut crop for money to purchase their winter shoes and coats and the school books for their children. Mr. Scott would buy literally tons of chestnuts that the residents would bring into the store every fall. In 1914, for example, receipts show that the Southern Express Company shipped out more than 9000 pounds of chestnuts that had been hauled by wagon from the store in Mayberry to the Railway Depot in Stuart.

Inside of the Mayberry Store building, one can still see upright braces that extend from the tops of the counters to the ceiling above. Coy Yeatts said that Mr. Scott put those uprights in there because he became concerned when the weight of the chestnuts stored in the room above the store began causing the ceiling to sag. Others have said that the braces were put there because of the way the floor in the room above the store would bounce when they were having square dances up there. I'm guessing that both stories are true and that the braces solved both of those problems.

There is one thing for sure, and that is when the blight killed the American chestnut trees in the Blue Ridge Mountains, it was a serious blow to the economy of Mayberry and all of the area around it. The chestnut blight actually started in New York around 1900, but it did not begin affecting the Blue Ridge Mountains of Virginia until about 1920. For a few years, there was an exceptional demand for the chestnuts that were continuing to grow in some unaffected regions of the mountains after they had been wiped out in the Midwest and Northeast. Eventually though, the blight reached everywhere in the country, including Mayberry, killing all of the chestnut trees in a period of just a few years. According to many local people, the chestnut blight delivered a more serious blow to the Mayberry economy than the one delivered by the Great Depression.

The sudden demise of the chestnut trees was such a disaster for Mayberry that some folks thought it surely must be a warning of the approach of the end of time. One Mayberry resident who apparently believed that to be the case was Mr. Simon Scott, who began passing out *Watchtower* tracts and warning everyone who would listen that "the end was nigh." Some people took him seriously and became quite repentant, at least for a while. Others reckoned that, while the end of time might be at hand for some folks, the rest of them were just too busy to worry about it.

Because of Ceph Scott's mercantile system of buying products from the local farmers, the Mayberry Store would sometimes run low on hard cash. Whenever that happened, Mr. Scott would issue payment for goods he bought using a form "scrip," also known as a "due bill," basically a hand written note that could be exchanged for a specified value in merchandise from the store. The use of scrip as currency was especially common during chestnut season, when the sales to the store were especially robust. In Mayberry at least, S.C. Scott's scrip was considered to be at least as sound as the United States dollar.

One of the many things that the "old folks," liked to recall when reminiscing about the old store was the large platform weighing scale that was located between the main store and the old storehouse. We know that S.C. Scott did a lot of dealing in livestock, and the ability to accurately weigh animals was essential to that kind of trade. But when the scale was not being used to weigh hogs or cattle, anyone who happened by was welcome to use it to weigh themselves and maybe their kids as well. For folks who had no access to a scale at home, this was a pretty big deal. But then as now, there were some people in Mayberry who would never have weighed themselves in public, even though most of them rarely had an opportunity to do much overeating.

Sooner or later, all of the sheep and cattle bought by the Mayberry Store were sent off to market, but every fall, many of the hogs that were bought were butchered right near the store by hired workers. Mr. Scott built a smokehouse behind the store to preserve the meat, and the quality of the smoked hams and side meat that he sold was legendary. For many years of the store's existence, smoked and cured hams and sides of bacon could be found hanging from the ceiling in the rear part of the store. In those days, all meat sold in a country store such as the one in Mayberry had to have been either smoked, salt cured, or canned.

It was impossible, of course, for Ceph Scott to anticipate and stock everything his customers' needed. But any time someone would ask for an item the store did not have, he would give that customer a quiet apology. "I'm sorry, but we don't have that right now," Ceph would tell them, and then quickly add, "but I can get it for you in just a few days."

Until the nineteen twenties, all of the transfer of goods between Mayberry and the nearest towns, mainly Stuart, Virginia, and Mount Airy, North Carolina, was conducted by horse and wagon. We even know the names of a few of those early wagoners. Abe Webb and Jasper Hensley were two of the men who drove their teams up and down the mountain on the two day trips to and from town, spending one night of each trip sleeping in their wagons. There were two young brothers in Mayberry, Prentice and Garver Reynolds, who began operating a regular freight hauling service between Scott's Store and Stuart Mercantile when they were barely in their teens. One may think of covered wagons as being primarily associated with the Old West, but they were used to haul freight everywhere in the country until well into the nineteen hundreds, including up and down the mountain to and from Mayberry.

One of the big events at the Scott Store was the weekly arrival of the *The Atlanta Constitution,* a newspaper to which S. C. Scott was a long time subscriber. The arrival of the constitution at the store was a much anticipated event, even though it usually came to Mayberry several days late. Other than the *Stuart Enterprise*, which was not especially informative about events of national and international importance, the *Constitution* was Mayberry's main source of news about the outside world. The paper was read so thoroughly by the customers at the store that it sometimes was literally worn through by the time it had completed its rounds. Not everyone in Mayberry agreed with the political bent of the *Constitution* though, and the store often echoed with lively discussions about the major issues of the day.

The international news provided by the *Constitution* apparently had a profound effect on some Mayberry residents. One member of the community, Elam Reynolds, named his own son *Oyama Karoganogi*, a name he claimed to have originally belonged to a hero in the in Russo-Japanese war of 1904. Mr. Reynolds had kept up with that distant conflict through his regular reading of the Atlanta paper. Fortunately for the son, he was just known as *Amur* when a youngster in Mayberry, and he then became known to his associates as O.K. Reynolds, once he left the area.

An example of just how heated the political discussions at the store could sometimes become can be shown by at least one disagreement that occurred there. A fellow from down near the Dan River by the name of Daniel Powell, got in a heated discussion with an itinerant barber who was cutting hair in the back of the store. The issue between the barber and Powell was said to be about the womens' right to vote, a highly divisive topic in 1910. Powell became so enraged that he jumped off the barber's stool and began beating the barber with his cane. The barber attempted to escape the confrontation by running out of the store, but Powell, with the barber's cloth still tied around his neck, pursued him out through the door, still flailing at him with the cane. Everyone who was there agreed that it was an obvious act of self-defense when the barber, a much smaller man than the Powell fellow anyway, suddenly turned around, pistol in hand, and shot Mr. Powell dead. The barber, whose name no one seemed to know, is supposed to have left Mayberry for Ohio. Whatever law enforcement that may have existed in Mayberry at the time did not choose to pursue or even indict the nameless barber. Now does that sound like your television Mayberry?

In many ways, the Mayberry Store was the recreational center of the Mayberry Community, or at least it was for the men. In the nineteen twenties and thirties, competitions in activities as diverse as marbles, horseshoes, and rifle and pistol shooting were often held near the store, and were said to be well attended. Another of the major

39

competitive events was the Saturday afternoon marble tournaments, held strictly for adult men. Does not the thought of grown men in overalls, crawling around in the dirt and dust, seriously shooting marbles not conjure up some incredible images? There were even rumors that some of the on-lookers at those contests would place wagers on the outcomes. I was shocked, shocked to hear that.

One of the things that made Mayberry such an interesting place was the collection of remarkable characters who lived in the community and frequented the Mayberry Store. Some of those folks were accused of spending more time piddling around the store than they spent at their homes. There have been many interesting stories told about the colorful customers from the time when Ceph Scott was running the store, and the following are some of my favorites. These stories were passed on to me by long-departed residents who personally knew these people and had observed them in action.

Dr. Davy

One of the regulars at the store for the first few decades of the nineteen hundreds was David Robertson, the Mayberry doctor. Although Dr. Davy, as he was called, never formally attended a day of medical school, he worked for several years as an assistant to Dr. John Martin, a formally trained medical doctor who had an office in the nearby community of Tobax. Through concentrated study and his several years of experience with Dr. Martin, David

Robertson was able to pass the state examination that certified him as a Doctor of Medicine, legally licensed to practice in the state of Virginia.

His preference for walking to see his patients and wearing overalls while on his rounds let his family and his neighbors know that none of this medical learning had made him feel that he was any different than rest of the good folk of Mayberry. Dr. Davie, as most folks called him, was a small man, and he spoke with a high pitched, excited voice that seemed to carry for miles. Folks walking along Mayberry Road could hear him lecturing to the loafers in Mayberry Store before they were close enough to see the building.

He had his causes, and one of the most important to him was regularity. He was perpetually concerned about "con-ste-pation," as he would emphasize it. He believed that it was a common source of all kinds of disease, and for Dr. Davy, it was the source of ailments for which he just happened to have effective treatments, mostly laxatives. "Con-ste-pation is the main cause of appendicitis," he would declare. "And it causes many other problems as well, including psoriasis, phlebitis, lumbago, sciatica, arthritis, neuritis, and neuralgia." Of course, a lot of the folks in Mayberry didn't know exactly what all those complaints were, but they were impressed that Dr. Davy seemed to know the cause and the cure for them all.

In the cause of maintaining a healthful diet, he was a man ahead of his time. While holding court around the Mayberry Store, he would sometimes use his long walking staff to point to a child eating candy and lecture him or her real good. "What are you eating that junk for, child? Don't you know it ain't no good for you? Git yourself some raisins or some apples." Ceph Scott, the proprietor, would sort of scowl and mumble to himself as he worked behind the counter. The store had raisins only around Christmas time and everybody had apples at home, but he had lots of candy in the store all of the time. But Mr. Scott knew that, on the balance, the presence of Dr. Davie holding fourth in his store was good for business.

Aunt Jule:

One truly incredible character who would put in an occasional appearance at the store was Julia Boswell. From the brogan shoes she wore under her long black skirts, to the pipe she often had clenched in her almost toothless mouth, Aunt Jule, as she was called, was a living image of the classical old-time mountain granny woman.

Even in her eighties, Julia Boswell was very self-sufficient, growing a prolific vegetable garden, raising her own chickens and pigs, and cutting and splitting her own firewood. She would show up at the store about once a month, usually right after her twelve dollar Confederate widow's pension check had arrived.

Her purchases from the store were usually quite basic: sugar, flour, salt, coffee, matches, some pipe tobacco for herself, chewing tobacco for her grown son, Pink, and snuff for her daughter, Ethel. She couldn't buy too many groceries at one time, even if she had the money. Whatever she bought at the store, she had to carry home in a tow sack slung across her back, and it was more than a mile back to her cabin up in Kettle Hollow

Aunt Jule's visits to the store were a special occasion for many of the store's customers, for Jule was a noted story teller. Her tales could be both frightful and humorous, and when she would get wound up, they could get more and more bizarre. Jule's late husband had fought in some of the bloodiest campaigns of the civil war, and she could recall every detail of that awful conflict that he had passed on to her. Folks said that she could describe the battles of Saltville and Cloyd's Mountain and make you think that she had just been there, in the thick of it all herself. But she also liked to tell about incredible adventures which she claimed to have experienced right here in Mayberry.

One of Jule's favorite tales was about the time she decided to butcher her own, apparently very large, hog. When she first shot it between the eyes, it fell right over, but when she climbed astride and stuck her knife in the jugular vein to bleed it, the hog jumped up and tried to run away. There was nothing she could do but to grab the bleeding hog around the neck and hang on. She claimed to have ended up riding that hog for a mile down Hurricane Knob and into Mayberry Creek, with the hog bleeding so much that the creek was turned red all the way down to the Dan River. When the hog finally fell down dead, she cut it up right there on the creek bank and carried it back up to her cabin, each ham and slab of side meat, one hunk at a time.

Everyone knew that many of Jule's tales were pure fiction, but they loved to hear her tell them anyway. She might begin a story about a simple event such as unusual weather – maybe thunder in a snow squall – up on the hillside where she lived. But then the tale might turn to how the strange weather was warning her of an imminent visit from a "haint" (a ghost, something in which she fervently believed), and conclude with her almost being done in by a panther while she was fleeing from the haint. She could sometimes hold a dozen or more customers spellbound within the store for hours. Occasionally, in the winter, she would stay so late at the store that she would have to borrow a lantern to light her way back to her home.

Although she really had little to fear in Mayberry, Julia Boswell made no secret of the fact that she carried an ancient derringer in her apron pocket. She would allow, however, that "This here little ole' gun ain't much truck when it comes to dealin' with haints and panthers and sech." There was a rumor that Jule carried the pistol as protection against thieves because of the bag of gold coins she either carried in another pocket or kept hidden under the hearth in her cabin. She never denied the tales, but after she died, no bag of gold was ever found. The story was likely just local mythology, tales of the kind that folks in the mountains are so fond of creating. The cruel fact is, Julia Boswell lived her entire life in what would be described today as grinding poverty, but so far as anyone could tell, her situation in life did not make her unhappy in the least.

Steve:

Although Steve was the younger brother of Ceph Scott, the owner, that did not mean that he got any special consideration when came in the store to sell eggs. He was in the store about three days a week, usually complaining about how pitifully little he was being given for the eggs and how outrageously high the prices were on anything he wanted to buy. It was true that Steve and his family had to be careful with the money they earned from selling eggs, chickens, wool, butter, and an occasional calf, all of which they produced on their farm. But apparently Steve's wife, Drusilla, was the money manager in that household, because Steve was heard to complain, "First she taken the egg money, then she taken the wool money, and now she want the calf money."

Once, when Steve found that the price of a hoe at his brother's store was 10¢ higher than he had expected, he sagely observed to Ceph, "I can clearly see that you've gone into this store business for the purpose of making money."

Steve lived a simple life that allowed for few luxuries, but there was one decadent pleasure to which he would occasionally treat himself, and that was chocolate drops. Whenever Steve would collect his egg money from the store, he would carefully count it out and tuck it all away, but before snapping his coin purse shut, he would sometimes remove just one nickel. And when he plunked his nickel down onto the counter top, he did not even have to say what it was for. Everyone at the store knew that Steve wanted chocolate drops, a nickel's worth of those incomparable, bosom-shaped, dark chocolate delights with the white vanilla filling. A nickel won't buy you even a single piece of that kind of candy today, but in 1915, when chocolate drops at the Mayberry Store sold for 12 cents a pound, a nickel would buy about ten of those delicious treats.

As Steve leaned over the counter, eyeing the process with suspicious anticipation, Ceph Scott would carefully scoop chocolate drops from the glass show case and shake them into a little number 2 brown paper bag, fold the top over, and hand it to Steve. Steve would take his treasure around behind the chimney, almost to the rear of the store, where he was out of everyone's way and he could stand stock still in the middle of the empty aisle. There, shielded from any earthly distractions, his eyes half closed as though intoxicated with sensual joy, he would slowly nibble his way through one of the rare pleasures afforded by his Spartan life.

Alas, one sad morning in 1917, when Steve put down his nickel for the chocolate drops, Ceph had to inform his brother Steve that, due to wartime rationing, there were no longer any chocolate drops available. There was no chocolate candy to be had at the Mayberry Store or anywhere else, probably until the end of the war.

Steve was heart-broken at the news, displaying an intense reaction of pain and grief. "Oh, woe, woe is me!" he moaned, almost in tears. "Them evil Germans done takened away all the chocolate!"

Mayberry Calling

The first telephone service that came to Mayberry was a branch of the system established between Stuart and

Laurel Fork, Virginia, around 1915. The telephone lines followed the Danville-Wytheville Pike up the mountain from Stuart, and from switchboards at locations such as Ballard and Vesta, trunk lines provided telephone service to other nearby communities. The first telephone in Mayberry was installed in S.C. Scott's store, and he immediately put it to good use, calling in orders to Stuart Mercantile Company and using it to learn the prices of livestock before deciding whether it was a good time to go to the trouble and expense of having them driven to market.

Ceph Scott's extensive use of the telephone to conduct business may have been responsible for the legend that he had his own private telephone line built from Mayberry to Stuart, but it is unlikely that was the case. For one thing, it would have been an enormous expense for an individual to undertake, not to mention the legal issues and other difficulties of maintaining a right-of-way for a telephone line strung over twenty miles of mountainous terrain. It is true that S.C. Scott paid for a private line to be strung for the five mile distance from Mayberry to the switchboard in Vesta, Virginia

After S.C. Scott's Store had enjoyed almost three profitable decades, sometime around 1920, things began to go wrong. For one thing, a couple of men in Mayberry bought Model-T trucks and began buying livestock and hauling it directly to Christiansburg, cutting out the middle man. For many years, that man had been S.C Scott, but simply having a telephone connection was no longer a critical advantage, and S.C Scott soon went out of the livestock business altogether.

The closing of the Mayberry Post Office in 1922 seriously affected the store business. The post office being located in the store had brought in potential customers every day of the week, and now, all at once, the number of folks coming into the store dropped way down.

S.C. Scott had always been generous in allowing his customers to buy on credit, and it was becoming obvious that some of them could not pay him what was owed. It may have also been that Mr. Scott had not kept up with the changes in what people were buying and his stock had become out of date, but for whatever reason, the store became less and less profitable and began to build up debt, and in 1923, S.C. Scott had to sell some of his land holdings to pay off some of his creditors.

To further complicate matters, Ceph Scott's wife kicked him out of their house and took up with former postmaster and business partner, Charlie Harrell. Folks in Mayberry still debate over precisely what role Charlie Harrell may have played in creating Mayberry Store's financial problems, but S.C. Scott ended up living in a little room in the back of the store, with folks whispering about how he had taken to strong drink. He may actually have been taking some of the cure-alls from off the shelves of the store because of genuine illness, but it soon became obvious to everyone that the poor man's health was failing.

Ceph Scott's youngest daughter, Dorothy Scott Reynolds, once told me a touching story about a conversation she had with her father in the last year of his life. She was just a young girl then, and although her father was barely able walk even a short distance, he insisted that he and Dorothy go for a walk one evening. He told her he wanted to go up Mayberry Road to see how the construction of the new Presbyterian Church was coming along. Cephas Scott had a special interest in that church, since he was the one who had donated the land on which it was being built.

As father and daughter walked up the hill beside the church, Mr. Scott became very short of breath and told his daughter that he needed to stop and rest. A large oak tree had been cut in the process of clearing for the construction of the church, leaving a stump large enough that they both could sit on it. Dorothy said they sat there beside the church for a long while, just enjoying the pleasant evening and listening to the call of a whippoorwill. Finally her father spoke. "I love this spot right here more than any place on this Earth." he told her. "And right over there," he said, pointing with his cane toward a small grove of trees behind the church, "is where I want to be buried."

Less than a year later, in August 1926, when Samuel Cephas Scott passed away, that is the spot where he was laid to rest. When the Parkway came through in 1937, the new road was built uncomfortably close to the church, but care was taken to leave the grave of S.C. Scott undisturbed. The grave is there today, beneath a solitary headstone in a grove of trees and enclosed by a chestnut rail fence, just up the hill and about a hundred feet to the west of Mayberry Presbyterian Church.

Charlie Harrell tried to keep the store going for a while after Ceph Scott had passed away, but times were hard in Mayberry and rumors were rife, making a lot of folks reluctant to trade with the man. Ceph Scott's widow and Charlie Harrell had gained possession of most of Ceph's property, including the store, but the store could not be made profitable at that time. Just a couple of years following the death of S.C. Scott, the remaining stock of goods was auctioned off, the windows were shuttered, and the doors of the Mayberry Store were locked for the next six years.

The Ceph Scott house in 2013.
It was built in 1905.

Yeatts Brothers' Store

When the Mayberry Store reopened in 1934, most folks viewed it as a hopeful sign. Like the rest of the country, Mayberry was just trying to dig out of the Great Depression, and after the store had been closed for so many years, many doubted that it would ever open again. The folks in Mayberry really had missed their store, and when it reopened, people thought that maybe times really were getting better. In fact, they were going to get a lot better in just a short time, but almost no one anticipated the economic boom that was about to happen in Mayberry.

Just a few months after the Yeatts Brothers reopened the Mayberry Store, work began on the City of Danville Hydroelectric Power Project. The project was one of the Roosevelt Administration's WPA depression-fighting efforts created to boost employment, but it was also built to provide both flood control for Kibler, Virginia, and electric power for Danville. It involved building two dams across the river in the Dan River George, one of them very close to Mayberry, and building an electric power generating plant farther down the Dan River in Kibler, Virginia.

Mayberry Road, which ran right past the store, provided the main access to the construction site for the lower of the two dams and for a part of the pipeline that would carry the water to the power plant in Kibler. One result of the project was the traffic on Mayberry Road increasing by a factor of ten for the next three years. It also meant that soon there were many more men working in Mayberry, and they were being paid decent wages. Families in Mayberry who had or could create a spare room began providing room and board for workers who came in from outside the area to work on the project. All of this activity further increased the flow of cash into the community and increased the demand for store-bought goods.

Everyone thought that, with an electric power generating plant so close by, Mayberry would surely soon be getting electricity. But all of the power lines from the project went straight to Danville, Virginia, and not one little electrical wire was ever connected to Mayberry. The good news, however, was that the Mayberry economy was about to receive another boost.

About the time that the City of Danville project began ramping down, construction on the Blue Ridge Parkway through the area started up, and the building of the section of the Parkway from Fancy Gap to Rocky Knob provided even more new jobs and more hard currency. While the years from 1934 to 1939 were still depression years for much of the country, those were probably the best economic times Mayberry has ever seen, before or since.

One of the first changes made after Coy Yeatts began operating the store was the installation of a gasoline pump with an underground storage tank. With all of the construction traffic on the Mayberry Road, fuel for all those cars and trucks was bound to be in big demand. The brand of gasoline initially sold at the Mayberry store was Standard Oil, but when Coy Yeatts' brother-in-law, Bud Hopkins, became the Gulf Oil distributor in Stuart, Virginia, the store quickly switched over to Gulf.

From 1934 until about 1952, whenever a customer would pull up in front of the store to buy gasoline, it would be delivered to the vehicle through a manually powered pump. The gasoline pump was enclosed in a tall, orange-colored pedestal made of steel, which had a long vertical handle attached to its side and a cylinder-shaped glass tank mounted near the top. A round glass globe mounted on the very top above the clear glass tank proclaimed in big orange letters that the pump was there to dispense *GULF* gasoline. Of course, a hand operated gasoline pump was a necessity at the Store until electric power finally did come to Mayberry.

For those who cannot remember that far back, the old hand-powered gasoline pumps with the ten gallon clear glass tank at the top required that the gasoline be pumped from the storage tank beneath the ground up and into the tank before it could be released into the vehicle through the hose and nozzle. The long vertical handle on the side of the pump was alternately pushed and pulled back and forth to pump the gasoline into the clear tank at the top. It was great fun to watch the red-orange liquid, first sloshing into the glass tank at the top of the pump, and later disappearing from the glass tank and into the vehicle sitting below it. Once the tank at the top of the pump had been pumped full, the procedure for delivering the gas into the tank was much the same as it is today

Safety was not that much of a consideration back then; the flow through the nozzle on the end of the hose would not automatically cut off if the car's tank became full (something that didn't happen much in Mayberry anyway). And one could not help but notice but that often a vehicle that stopped to buy gas at the Mayberry Store would have a rag stuffed into the filler neck of its gasoline tank instead of the original tight-fitting gas cap.

One day Grandpa decided that I appeared to be having so much fun just watching customers buying their gas that maybe I should be helping out as well. I could not be trusted to dispense the gasoline into the cars, of course, so he assigned me the job of pushing and pulling the pump handle to fill the top of the pump up with the gas. I was just a small kid at the time, but I can tell you that pumping gas to the top of one of those old contraptions took a lot of effort. The tank at the top one of those old pumps held ten gallons, and when someone pulled up in a vehicle such as a gravel truck and requested a fill-up, the twenty or more gallons it could take required about ten minutes of hard pumping.

Tabs with numbers one through ten were mounted on a rod that ran up on the inside of the clear tank. The numbers ran from the top down, so it was always easiest to keep track of the amount of gas dispensed if you started with the pump tank full. The application of some mental math was usually required anyway, since most people who pulled up to the pump would tell the keeper of the pump, "Gimme' 'bout a dollar's worth." That would have been about five gallons in those days.

**The Gasoline Pump that stood in front of Yeatts Brothers'
Store in the thirties and forties.** (Courtesy of L. H. Hutchins)

At the Mayberry Store that I can remember, that still-important petroleum product, kerosene, was being dispensed from a green steel tank with a rotary hand pump mounted on top. In nineteen forty-nine, a gallon of kerosene cost about a dime and the price of a gallon of the one grade of gasoline sold at the store was twenty cents, period, with none of this 19.9 cents per gallon nonsense in the Mayberry of the forties.

The Mayberry store was even more dependent on kerosene for a source of energy than the rest of the community. Not only did the store use kerosene lamps to provide interior lighting, but the soft drinks were kept cool (sort of) and the butter was kept semi-solid by the kerosene powered refrigerator in the store. In case you are wondering, ice cream was unavailable at the Mayberry store until sometime after electricity arrived. The kerosene refrigerator could barely keep soda pop cool enough to drink, and keeping ice cream frozen was far beyond its capabilities.

Although the drinks kept in the kerosene refrigerator in the Mayberry Store were never as cold as most folks would have liked, that was probably more the result of the owners' trying to conserve kerosene than the inability of the refrigerator to maintain a lower temperature, had it been turned to a lower setting. Between the kerosene lamps that lighted the place and that old kerosene refrigerator gurgling away, my childhood memory of the old store is mostly one of the dimly-lit, tunnel-like room that smelled strongly of kerosene.

Sometime in the early nineteen fifties, an electric gasoline pump was installed in addition to the manually powered one. A second gasoline storage tank had been placed under the ground beside the store, and "high test" gasoline now became available. The reason high octane gasoline was developed in the first place was to keep the engines in the newer cars from "knocking," a pre-ignition problem that could, over time, damage the newer high compression engines. Using the more expensive "high test" gasoline in the lower compression engines of older cars was of no benefit at all, but you couldn't convince tell some folks of that. There were (and probably still are) those who believed that it had to be good for the old flivver if, every once in a while, they treated her to a tankful of high test gasoline. They thought it kind of cleaned'er out.

In the seventies, when the petroleum distributor that supplied the Mayberry Store changed its affiliation from Gulf brand petroleum products to Marathon, the store had to change too. The brand name on the gasoline pumps out front were changed to read MARATHON, but the round orange GULF sign beside the store remained. It is still there today, and I am told that the proprietor frequently gets offers from customers who want to buy the *Gulf* sign.

For as long as Coy O. Yeatts ran the store, there was no self-service, meaning the gasoline was always dispensed either by him or someone else working for the store. Later, when Addie Wood took over the operation, an electric power switch was installed inside the store that the proprietor could allow the self-service sale of gasoline while maintaining a modest level of security.

During the past century of operation, the array of merchandise stocked by the store would have changed significantly. In the earliest days of the store's operation, a much simpler time, it mostly carried really basic stuff: hardware, staple grocery items, household supplies, work clothes, and such. My earliest memories go back to around the end of World War II, and the inventory I can recall from that time was mostly staple goods, but also a lot of candy, soft drinks, and tobacco products. I can recall when there was one long shelf on the wall behind the counter which was completely filled with different brands of tobacco. Several of the many brands of plug-type chewing tobacco sold there are still clear in my mind. Black Maria, Bull Durham, Bull of the Woods, Brown's Mule, Day's Work, and several others were all on that shelf.

Several brands of snuff were also displayed on the same shelf as the chewing tobacco. A few of the snuff brands I can remember are Tube Rose, Railroad Mills, Rooster, and Square, with Tube Rose being by far the most popular. That popularity may have been because the large size container of Tube Rose Scotch Snuff came in such lovely glass drinking glasses. Also, attached to Tube Rose containers were coupons that could be exchanged for valuable premiums. It was even whispered that some of the ladies in Mayberry used the small size Tube Rose Snuff tins as hair curlers. Tube Rose Snuff used to be so popular that just about everyone in Mayberry knew the *Tube Rose* ditty.

If your snuff's too strong, it's wrong,
Get Tube Rose, Get Tube Rose.
To make your life one happy song,
Get Tube Rose, Get Tube Rose.
With Tube Rose, believe you me,
You'll get gifts for free, free, free,
With coupons, with coupons,
In Tube Rose, in Tube Rose.

On the shelf right above the tobacco products resided an array of cure-alls and patent medicines: Carter's Liver

Pills, Black Draught, Lydia Pinkham's Women's Compound, Fletcher's Castoria, Swamp Root, Sloan's Liniment, and many more alleged curatives were all displayed there.

The glass candy cases that are still located on the top of the counter on the left side near the front door have been there ever since the store was built, although they are no longer used to display candy. I can well remember some of the kinds of candy kept in those cases in the forties though, especially my favorites: licorice babies, orange slices, and marshmallow peanuts.

The soft drinks that were kept in that old kerosene refrigerator did not include many of the brands you might expect to find in a drink cooler today. The brands of soda that I recall in the refrigerator were *Red Rock Cola* and *Royal Crown Cola* (in lieu of Pepsi or Coke), *Nehi Grape*, *Bireleys Orange*, and *YooHoo* chocolate soda. Someone would occasionally come into the store and ask for a "dope," which indicated that they wanted to buy a *Coca-Cola,* but in Mayberry they would have to have made do with either a Red Rock or a Royal Crown.

The store was always well stocked with bubble gum, the one treat that Coy Yeatts would give to his nieces and nephews when they would come there. He often gave a piece of Bazooka Bubble Gum to each member of our tribe of cousins when we would come trooping into the store, simply because he knew how much that would aggravate his sisters. The mothers of us kids were a group of women who, although they could not agree on what day of the week it was, were all united in their hatred of bubble gum.

My strongest memories of the Mayberry Store span the years from the end of the Second World War (1945) until about the end of the fifties. Summer Saturdays were the best times to be there. That was the time that the store would have the largest number of loafers "hanging around," and it also happened to be when my cousins and I would have an opportunity to spend the most unsupervised time there.

I have to completely rely on second-hand stories about the characters who frequented the store back when it was run by Cephas Scott, since they were all long gone by the times I can recall. I can actually remember many of the loafers from the Mayberry Store from the time when Coy Yeatts was running it, and I was actually there when a couple of these interesting incidents happened.

John

Dr. Davie's son, John, spent most of his waking hours – and quite a few of his sleeping ones – at the Mayberry Store. John had been a very hard worker as a young man, but in his retirement, he spent much of his time just loafing around, usually at the store. He spent so much of his time there that his sister, Jettie, who kept house for her brother some of the time, would occasionally walk over to the store just to check and be sure that her brother was still among the living.

One of the things about John that made him readily recognizable was his constantly disheveled state of dress. One might have mistaken John for a street person, had there been such a thing in Mayberry. He wore many layers of muddy and rumpled clothing, and the strings of the oversized brogans he always wore were never tied.

In his later years, John seemed to reserve most of his energy for making moonshine. John was generally known in Mayberry as a dependable source of hooch, but the quality of the booze he could supply was apparently somewhat erratic. Depending upon whom you asked, John was said to make either "pretty good stuff" or accused of making "stuff that'll eat your guts out." That may have simply been different reactions to essentially the same product.

John was known to have had a small still located somewhere nearby, and the revenuers probably would have had little difficulty locating it, had they been so inclined. The Federal ATF Agents, the official professional "revenooers," were not all that interested in a little, local hobby still like John's when they out were scouting for illegal liquor production. So long as nobody was being poisoned, they were mainly interested in the larger, more commercial operations, leaving the search for small-time moonshine operations like John's up to the local gendarmes.

The couple of times that the county sheriff had located and chopped up John's still, he had always been sufficiently forewarned, so that he was nowhere around when the raid occurred. But one day, when communications apparently broke down, the sheriff and a couple of deputies were able to surprise John just as he was finishing up running off a batch. The officers gave the Commonwealth's Attorney a sworn affidavit that they had observed John actually in the process of filling a jar and placing it in a case with several other similar jars, all of them found to be filled with illegal booze.

John later described his ordeal to the folks at the store. "When the Sheriff stepped out of the bushes and hollered that I was under arrest, John lamented, "the only thing I could think to do was just hold my breath 'til I died."

The officers placed John under arrest and took him to the county seat for arraignment. John did not have the $100 he needed for bail, but he was allowed to call the Mayberry Store and ask if there was anyone there who would bail him out. He also asked for someone to please get word to his sister, Jettie, so she would not worry about him, should he have to stay locked up in the county jail for a spell while he awaited trial.

It was Coy Yeatts who answered the telephone at the store when John called, and he assured John that he would get word to Jettie as soon as possible. That did not take long, because shortly after the call, Jettie walked into the store looking for her brother.

When Coy gave Jettie the message that John was in jail in lieu of a hundred dollar bond, she responded that she didn't have no hundred dollars, and if she did, she wouldn't use it to bail out John. Later though, she had a change of heart. "I sure do hate he's gonna' have to sit down there in that jail," she thought out loud, "but maybe now he'll have the time to keep his dang shoes tied."

Lloyd

Lloyd often helped John make his moonshine, and he was always happy to take his payment in product. He seldom showed up at the store during the week, but on Saturday afternoon, it was a common sight to see Lloyd come weaving down the Mayberry Road toward the store, obviously soused to the gills. He never caused any trouble though. He normally would just buy himself a Moon Pie and a bottle of soda pop, find a place to sit off by himself, and keep out of everyone's way. Usually, his presence at the store was hardly noticed.

One Saturday afternoon when Lloyd staggered into the store, however, he was looking mighty peaked. He walked over and propped himself up on the counter, then asked Coy, "You got anything for a bellyache? My belly's been hurtin' me somethin' terrible! Been hurtin' all day!

Although the Coy figured that Lloyds problem was because of something he had been drinking, he was sympathetic with Lloyd's complaint. He occasionally suffered digestive difficulties of his own, and the store was now stocking a new medication, one promoted as a cure for what was now being called *acid indigestion.* Several of the folks at the store had tried the new medication and all had declared that *Alka-Seltzer* was good for all kinds of ailments, especially the bellyache. The foil packet had yet to be invented, so *Alka-Seltzer* back then came packaged in glass tubes; either a short tube containing eight tablets for a quarter, or the tall economy-size tube of twenty tablets that sold for fifty cents. Coy Yeatts handed Lloyd a small tube which had already been opened, but still contained several of the quarter-sized white tablets. "Here," he told Lloyd, "why don't you try of a couple of these. They're supposed to work real good and they'll be on the house."

Lloyd gratefully accepted the tube and immediately weaved over to the refrigerator where he extracted a bottle of 7-*Up* soda. As Lloyd pried the cap off of his soda, everyone in the store was kind of watching and wondering what he was going to do next and Lloyd did not disappoint them. Tucking his drink into the crook of his arm, he screwed the top off of the tube of *Alka-Seltzer* and shook three or four of the tablets out into his palm. Then, before anyone could advise him to the contrary, he popped them into his mouth, all of them at once.

The regulars were all staring at Lloyd, not quite believing what he was doing, but no one made a move to stop him. Lloyd chomped down on the tablets a few times and tried to swallow them dry, then finally succeeded in washing them down by chugging his 7-Up.

Lloyd just stood there for a couple of minutes, bracing himself against the refrigerator, with his eyes sort of bugging out. He kept opening his eyes wider and wider as he staggered toward the front of the store, where he thumped the empty bottle down and propped up against the counter as he searched in his pockets for the money to pay. As he plopped his dime down on the counter, Lloyd shook his head and patted himself on the tummy. "Oh, Lordy-mercy-me," he declared to no one in particular. "Them-there things sure is a-carryin' on in there."

As he wobbled out through the front door of the store, Coy wanted to know if Lloyd was going to be all right, but Lloyd, after giving a mighty belch, insisted that he was just fine. And the next Saturday, Lloyd was right back there at the store, this time proclaiming his own sincere testimonial to the miraculous healing power of *Alka-Seltzer*.

Harlow:

Known as a rather tough character in his younger years, Harlow had once pulled some hard time for severely cutting another man in a fight. That had happened years before, and although he seemed to be mostly lazy and harmless as an older man, he continued to carry the label of someone who was not to be trifled with. Even with his prison record, he had been able to find work guarding convicts for the county at a time when there was a lot of highway construction in the area and good help had temporarily been hard to find. Some said that the county hired him as a guard because both the sheriff and the convicts knew he would not hesitate to shoot dead any prisoner who might try to escape.

A family affliction of hereditary glaucoma began to destroy his eyesight when he was still a fairly young man, however, and that put an end to his potential for most employment. He attended the state school for the blind for a time, where he learned some manual crafts such as making dippers from coconut hulls and assembling leather belts and purses. Even with his impaired eyesight he was somehow able to walk the half-mile shortcut from his home to the

Mayberry Store, walking across open fields and through woodlands, even crossing a creek and climbing over several fences.

Harlow spent a lot of time sitting outside at the front of the store, usually in a place where the sunlight was bright enough that he could see well enough to whittle. It may have been that he liked to whittle as a way of displaying his large ornate lock-blade knife and reminding everyone that he was a man with a past.

Sometimes, Harlow would get up and kind of feel his way around the side of the store, on around past back of the store and into a thicket of rhododendron, the hiding place where he kept his jar of moonshine. No one ever dared to bother Harlow's liquor, even though he always kept it in the same hiding place and never seemed to have any difficulty in locating the jar himself. It was fairly obvious that something in addition to poor eyesight sometimes made it difficult for Harlow to negotiate the terrain around the store.

Earnest:

Earnest would buy himself a brand new pair of bibbed overalls every spring. He was very particular about his overalls, though, and was not willing to settle for just any old kind of denim britches. He had a strong preference for Lee Brand Overalls.

Lee Overalls were known to be sturdy and long-wearing, and they had useful pockets all over the place, many of them well-designed for special purposes. Like most overalls, they had the snap-close chest pocket in the center of the bib, a properly secure place to carry cash, for those who happened to have any. They also had the little pocket with a slash opening located right at the bottom of the bib, the perfect place for Earnest to stash the little hammerless Harrington and Richardson revolver he always carried.

The other pockets – the pencil pocket on the bib, two slash pockets on the sides, the two hip patch pockets, the tool pockets on the leg, and the watch pocket on the waist – all were pretty much standard for every brand of overalls. But most brands of overalls did not have that perfectly-designed little pocket at the bottom of the bib like the Lee Brand. Earnest was not a big fellow, but folks in Mayberry knew not to mess with him just the same. Some folks think that maybe this Earnest was the persona upon whom another, more famous Earnest from another Mayberry was based.

One blustery March day, Earnest came striding purposefully into the store and without greeting or comment, followed the long side counter all of the way to the back of the store, the place where the men's work clothing was kept. There, on the counter top, flanked by the blue chambray shirts, the overall jackets, and the dungarees, was a brand-new stack of bibbed blue denim overalls. A quick examination of the stack, however, revealed to Earnest that these were not what he had expected to find. All he could find was Anvil Brand overalls.

"Hey Coy!" Earnest shouted out to the store keeper. "Where's your dad-blamed Lee Overhauls?"

"Uh, we don't have Lee brand anymore, Earnest. We've started carrying just the Anvil Brand," Coy explained.

"That's what most folks have been asking for of late. They went up on the price of Lees, and they tell me that Anvil's actually better made."

Earnest spread a pair of Anvil Brand overalls out on the counter, front side up and began a careful, detailed scrutiny. There was the required little slash pocket near the bottom of the bib, but it had a double opening, it wasn't at quite the right angle, and it wasn't quite deep enough either.

Coy walked over until he was right across the counter from Earnest and began to describe the virtues of his Anvil Brand products. "That Anvil fabric may feel softer than the Lee, but it is really tougher," he claimed. "And most fellers really like the new zipper fly. All of the brands are changing over to a zipper fly." Coy then demonstrated just how easily the zipper fly on Anvil Brand operated.

A zippered fly on a pair of overalls? What was the world coming to? Earnest just didn't trust them zippers. He much preferred the totally reliable metal buttons like those that securely closed the fly on the Lee overalls like the ones he had worn all of his adult life. He really did need a new pair of overalls, but if he had to, he knew he could walk the three miles out to Meadows of Dan to get exactly what he wanted from Tom Agee's Store. But Earnest was not one to rush to judgment.

Earnest carefully unzipped the fly of the pair of Anvil Brand overalls he had spread out on the counter in front of him. The zipper zipped the fly open smoothly and easily, with no hint of sticking. Then he zipped them back up. No problem. Open. Closed. Open. Closed. The zipper seemed reliable enough, but that was when they were new. How long would a zipper fly hold up? This required some serious thought, an analysis of all the advantages and disadvantages of such a significant change. Finally he made his decision.

"You know," Earnest announced, as he folded up the pair of overalls he had been examining and placed it back on the stack, "that-there zipper fly is **just too damned convenient**." Then he turned and thumped out of the store.

One thing you might have noticed, anytime you might have ventured into *Yeatts Brothers' Store,* would have been the musical instruments scattered all around. There usually would have been an old banjo propped up in a chair somewhere, an old guitar laying on its back on a counter top, and an old fiddle, hanging from a piece of twine looped over a nail in the wall. Dump Yeatts played the fiddle when he was a younger man, and Coy could play pretty good claw hammer banjo, but both were too shy to play if there were many folks around to hear them.

Sometimes though, "Babe" Dudley Spangler or Len Reynolds might take that old fiddle down from the wall, tune it up, and begin to play *Cumberland Gap* or *Ida Red*. Once in a while, Ace Spangler just might show up and join in on the guitar. If Harry Pendleton happened by and picked up the banjo, then that old store would come alive with traditional mountain music of a kind you hardly ever hear anymore.

The poster advertising Charlie Monroe's *Big Radio Show* when it came to Mayberry. No one remembers there ever being a "Junior League" anywhere near Mayberry.

Charlie Monroe:

Charlie Monroe did not really spend a lot of time at the Mayberry Store, but he was surely there for one memorable visit. In November of 1938, Charlie Monroe brought his "Big Radio Show," complete with Bill and Zeke, to Mayberry. Posters and handbills were distributed all around Mayberry, Meadows of Dan, Laurel Fork, and Bell Spur announcing the event.

The show was scheduled to begin at 7:30 P.M. on November 22, 1938, at the Mayberry School. But it seems there was a problem with that plan. The Mayberry School had closed down a few months earlier, and for reasons on which even the folks who can remember the performance are unable to agree, Charley and Company were told at the last minute that they could not use the school building. They were, however, allowed to borrow some benches from the Mayberry Presbyterian Church. The men who had come early to see the show were recruited to carry the benches borrowed from the church down Mayberry Road a just little ways. The show could go on, but it was going to be performed the fertilizer shed beside Yeatts Brothers' Store instead of in the school building.

The people who were there estimated that a crowd of over sixty showed up for the performance, and that was a really large crowd, considering the size of the building. But again, the men had gotten busy and moved most of the feed and fertilizer out of the building. They even cobbled up a little makeshift stage, made by laying boards across stacks of sacks of fertilizer. They somehow arranged the benches in the shed so that thirty or forty people could be seated and still leave room for about twenty more standing around the wall. Several more folks were jammed onto the little porch, listening to the performance through the open door from outside the building. But the production, having no amplification and no electric lighting, was completely dependent upon strong voices and kerosene lamps.

There have been many exciting tales told about what happened that night, some of them a lot more plausible than others. But we can start with the known fact that Monroe Brothers, Bill and Charlie, did not get along very well. It is also a matter of record that older brother Charlie, who was the more famous of the two at the time, thought that he should be the star of the show and that everyone else should defer to him. Many folks thought that Bill was the superior musical talent, however, and that Charlie was deliberately keeping his brother in the background. If you will give a close look at the poster advertising the Mayberry event, it is easy to see why Bill would have been incensed when he saw it. A serious altercation between the Monroe Brothers is supposed to have occurred that night in Mayberry, with the results that Charlie was the only Monroe brother to perform in Mayberry and the Monroe Brothers never performed together again.

The story makes more sense if one looks at the history of the brothers and their intense rivalry. And it is also a fact that many outstanding musicians performed with Bill

Monroe for a time, but soon left the Bluegrass Boys to go their own way. One might conclude that neither Bill Monroe nor Charlie were easy people to work with.

In spite of all the problems that occurred that night, everything said about the show indicated that it was great entertainment and everyone felt that they had gotten their full twenty-five cents worth. For the folks of Mayberry, to see Charlie Monroe and hear him play *You're Gonna' Miss Me When I'm Gone* and *Bringing in the Georgia Mail,* live and in person, was a treat beyond description.

The comedy skit, a blackface minstrel act which would definitely not be considered acceptable today, was said to be the funniest thing anyone there had ever seen. In fact, it was so funny that one little guy, sitting at the end of the front row bench, laughed so hard that he wet his pants. As the effect of his laughter ran down the bench, the folks sitting farther down the bench jumped up, one after the other, as their seats were wetted. When the rest of the audience realized what was happening on the front row, it just added to their enjoyment of the show.

Barnstorming with a musical show was probably not an easy way to get rich in the 1930's. With the cost of admission at 15¢ for kids and 25¢ for adults, plus selling a few records for 50¢ each, the entire take for Charlie Monroe's Big Radio Show in Mayberry that evening must have been something less than twenty dollars.

Lee:

Richard did not yet have his driver's license, but his dad would sometimes allow him to drive the family car for short excursions around Mayberry. These would just be short trips such as the half mile from their home near Mayberry Creek to the Mayberry Store, or the mile over to his Uncle Coy's house to visit the cousins. Sometimes, without telling his dad, he would drive down the Lower Dam Road to the pinnacle overlook. Within a few miles driving distance of Mayberry, there was little chance of ever encountering a law-enforcement officer, so long as one avoided driving on the Blue Ridge Parkway.

For as far back as I can remember, Uncle Neil seemed to always have the nicest, newest cars of anyone in our family. But that new nineteen and fifty-two DeSoto two-door hardtop with the "Firedome V-8" engine was really over the top – just about the sleekest, fanciest, gussied-up car that anyone in Mayberry had ever seen.

One summer Saturday afternoon, we were all surprised when our cousin Richard asked and Uncle Neil granted permission for Richard to drive a bunch of us cousins the short distance from Grandpa's house up Mayberry Road to Uncle Coy's Store. We all knew that Richard really wanted to go to the store to show off his Dad's new car, but we were all cool with that. We were just excited about the opportunity to take a ride in that fancy new car. We were also sure that Richard would fudge on his Dad's permission and drive on up to the Mayberry Church, turn around, then ease back down the road and pull the car over right in front of the store. We were just happy to be treated to all of the riding in that fancy car that we could get.

Richard drove the long route, just as we expected, turning around at the church before driving back and successfully parking the big car in the narrow space between the road and the loafer's bench at the store. It was a typical Saturday afternoon, with a lot of the Mayberry loafers hanging around, and, as was also typical of a Saturday afternoon, some of the folks out front had been thoroughly lubricating themselves with moonshine.

Uncle Coy strongly disapproved of alcohol, but a customer was a customer, so he tolerated a few drunks occasionally hanging around the store, as long as they caused no problems. There was a clear understanding between the customers who drank and Coy Yeatts that there would never be any open display of the alcohol, no foul language, and no boisterous behavior. They could sit on the bench in front and periodically go around in back of the store and take nips from the jar until they were crawling instead of walking, just so long as there was no disturbance.

We just sat there, reared back on the fat leather seats inside of the car in front of the store, just waiting for the customers to take notice of the new Desoto. After a while, a few of the more energetic guys got up and walked over to the car, then ambled around it, scrutinizing, admiring, and commenting on the vehicle.

In nineteen fifty-two, there were not all that many options available on a car, even an up-scale model like that one. That car had just about every accessory that could be ordered as original equipment. It had a radio and a heater, of course, and turn signals, which were still an option in the early fifties. It had come equipped with white-wall tires, mud flaps, outside rear-view mirrors, fog lights, and two-tone paint. And there were no roof pillars between the front and rear windows of the car. For some reason, now lost in history, the absence of the roof pillars was what caused a car to be designated as a hard-top.

This DeSoto car was also equipped with an option that I can recall ever seeing on only one or two other cars. The stalk that supported the driver's side rear-view mirror housed two small gauges – a thermometer and an altimeter. It was a safe bet that no one in Mayberry had ever seen a car tricked up with anything like that.

One of the more interested onlookers was Lee, a Mayberry resident who often spent a lot of his Saturday time at the store. Today, like most Saturdays, Lee appeared to be have been nipping at the fruit jar pretty heavily. He stumbled over to the car, then weaved around it two or three times, carefully scrutinizing it from top to bottom. Eventually, he approached the driver's window so Richard could fill him in on all of the details.

"Mighty nice car you got there, Richie," he addressed our cousin in the driver's seat. "I rekon it's your dads.

"Thanks. Yeh, it is my dad's, but I get to drive it a lot," Richard fibbed.

"Boy, hit's got 'bout ever thing they is on it, I rekon. White walls, radio, two-tone…," he walked around the car again, admiringly ticking off the features, one-by-one. But as came back around to the driver's window he adopted a puzzled expression, having just noticed the two gauges built in with the outside rear view mirror. "What's all that for?" he asked, pointing to the gauges.

Richard was more than happy to demonstrate his technological sophistication. "Well, this one here's a thermometer," he explained, pointing to one of the gauges, "and that other one there is an altimeter."

"Al-ti-me-ter?" queried the admirer. "I ain't never heard of that. What's uh al-ti-me-ter?"

"An altimeter is a gadget that tells how high you are," Richard innocently explained.

"You kiddin' me," responded Lee. "Boy, I could sure use one o' them things."

Lee then bent over toward the gauge until his face was just inches away. "Whew, whew, whoooo," he puffed onto the face of the gauge. "Now how high does it say?"

Fred:

When Coy Yeatts's youngest son, Fred, was just a young teenager, Coy began training him in the operation of the store. Fred was hard working and totally reliable, and he also had a lot of chores he had to do at home and on the farm. But when the weather was bad, Fred would be the one given the job of helping out at the store. When Coy needed to make a feed delivery, if Fred's grandfather, Dump Yeatts, could not be at the store, Fred might even be left in charge for a while.

For most of the store's long history, there was always a checkerboard somewhere around, usually placed on a nail keg located between two low, cane-bottomed chairs, all set up and ready for a match any time someone wanted to take on the challenge. The store's habitual loafers occupied the checkerboard much of the time, but when things got slow and no real customers were around, one of the local ringers might allow Fred to play him a game or two. It wasn't long before they found that Freddie was a really fast learner. A couple of the best players even began giving Fred some serious checker lessons, hoping that he would humiliate some of their rivals. Fred improved rapidly, and in a short time he was able to beat all but the very best of the Mayberry Store Checker Champions.

When fall came that year, all of Fred's time was taken up by the work he had to do at home, allowing the checker hierarchy at the Mayberry store to remain stable for a while. That winter, however, when fourteen year old Fred was able to return to playing checkers at the store, he immediately began mopping up on the local champions, one after the other. Some of the strategies Freddie was applying were unlike any known to the checker masters at the store, making them very suspicious. The situation, they decided, required an inside investigation.

By asking seemingly innocuous questions of some of Fred's brothers and sisters, the investigators learned that Fred had borrowed a book called *The Art of Draughts,* an English publication about the strategy of playing checkers, from the county library. When confronted by his accusers,

Freddie readily admitted reading the book to learn new strategies, but he had a most logical defense. His younger sister, Virginia, had been regularly thrashing him in the checker competition at home, and he really studied the book on checkers just to learn enough so that he could beat her. It was a matter of self-defense, he pleaded, and he didn't see anything wrong with that!

The old former checker champions at the Mayberry Store put their heads together for a serious discussion regarding the new challenge, and quickly reached their conclusion: Learning to play checkers from a book and then practicing what was learned, at home and in secret, was actually a form of cheating. Fred should therefore be banned from all further official checker competition in the store. Fred would be allowed to share his new strategies in games played just for fun, however, but they would not be considered official competition.

After a while, many of the store cronies simply got tired of playing checkers, with the outcomes almost certain before the games were even begun. That was when Gene Barnard brought a new game into the store; a game more dependent on luck and less dependent on skill than checkers. The game was called Monopoly, and it also had the advantage that, instead of just two participants at a time, the number who could play in a Monopoly Game was essentially unlimited. For several years, when the weather was bad and the loafers were forced inside, a game of Monopoly would continually be in progress. Sometimes the same game would continue for days, or even for weeks, as different players would have to leave and others would take their places.

That original Monopoly board, the very same old, well-worn game board that entertained the Mayberry Store regulars for over a decade, is still there on display in the Mayberry Trading Post.

In 1955 Fred finished high school and left his home in Mayberry for the U.S. Naval Academy, leaving Coy Yeatts with no sons to help out at home or at the store. There were four pretty daughters still living at home, but Coy would not consider allowing any of them to work in the store. He thought it wouldn't have been right to expose those young ladies to some of those characters who frequented the place. The locals who sat around in the store so much were doubtlessly harmless, but that didn't mean that they wouldn't ogle any young woman who set foot inside the store to the point of discomfort and embarrassment. But besides that, Coy's wife, Mary Lee, was in poor health and the girls' help was needed at home even more than in the store.

Coy O. Yeatts:

Coy Yeatts was himself something of an interesting character, very intelligent but also suspicious of change. All of his life he had been a very hard worker, but from his mid-forties on, he had been plagued with a serious back problem. The back injury, probably a ruptured disk, kept him in pain and frustrated at his inability to do the work he felt was essential for the store and his farm. Coy was always skeptical of the use of medication to relieve pain, but sometimes his back pain was so severe that his only relief was to take the medication and lie flat on his back.

Coy was someone who never cared much for television, much preferring to read, if ever he had any time to spare. But with Coy's wife ailing and Coy having to spend an increasing amount of time nursing his back, an older son, Charles, bought his folks a television set and had it installed in their home. Coy ignored the television at first, but eventually he began to watch it for short periods while he was resting his back.

One day, after Coy had been forced to spend the morning lying on the bed, nursing his hurting back and watching Dave Garroway on the *Today Show*, he was finally able to get up and make his way down to the store.

"Well, I'll have to admit that television is a great thing," he announced to everyone, as he painfully shuffled into the store. "If it wasn't for television, I would never have known about the wonders of a dancing pig."

Between Coy Yeatts' back problems and the fact that his father, J.H. (Dump) Yeatts was approaching ninety, there was a real need for some additional help in managing the store. In 1962, a local farm lady, Ms. Addie Wood, began helping Coy run the store, a partnership in which her responsibility increased with time. In 1966, the state of Virginia imposed its first general sales tax of 2%. Then in 1968, when the statewide rate was increased to 3% and a local sales tax of 1% was added as well, Coy decided that this tax business had just gotten too darn complicated.

Now nearing seventy, still suffering from his back, and kind of tired of the store business anyway, Coy Yeatts turned the store over to Miz Addie and retired.

The Mayberry Trading Post in 1982. That is former owner Coy O. Yeatts seated in front of the store.

The Mayberry Trading Post

When Addie Wood took over the operation of the Mayberry Store from Coy O. Yeatts, Coy's son, Coy Lee (it's confusing, I know), began assisting her in the store. Coy Lee, not coincidentally, was the husband of Miss Addie Wood's niece, Dale Wood Yeatts. A few years later, after she had retired from her job as an accountant Dale Yeatts began helping Coy Lee and Addie in the store.

With Addie Wood and Coy Lee now running the store, Yeatts Brothers Store was obviously no longer an appropriate name for the business. After some serious deliberation, Coy Lee and Addie decided to rename the store the Mayberry Trading Post, and they soon had signs on the store's front, side, and back displaying that new name.

A lot of things had changed in Mayberry in the years since Coy O. and J.H. Yeatts first started running the store. The population of Mayberry had been in a state of decline since World War II, and that certainly affected the business. Now that automobiles and roads been improved so much that a trip to town took a couple of hours instead of most of a day, a lot of folks in Mayberry were buying their groceries and hardware from the big stores in town. For years, local farmers had provided the store with a significant snack and lunch business, but with farming in the area also in a state of decline, that business was way down as well. The new store management decided that the future of the old store lay in its appeal to the tourist trade, so they began stocking more and more crafts and souvenirs, items selected for their appeal to the tourists who stopped in from off the Blue Ridge Parkway. In fact, it is doubtful that the Mayberry Store would even be in business today, if not for visitors who come into the store from the Blue Ridge Parkway. Fortunately for the Trading Post, as the local trade in household goods and staples at the store has declined, the interest in the historical old store shown by tourists and travelers on the Parkway has increased.

The store stocked up on the usual trinkets that tourists tend to buy; postcards, fairy stones, corncob pipes, poke bonnets, Mayberry tee-shirts, and such. Miss Addie and Coy Lee found that tapes and CD's of traditional mountain music, much of it recorded by talented local musicians, were very popular with visitors to Mayberry. The same thing was found to be true of books which emphasized the culture of the Appalachian Mountains, many of which were written by authors from the area. But for many years, the store's most popular merchandise has been the locally produced selection of home-made canned goods such as jams, preserves, molasses, pickles, and chow chow. If there is anything that folks who live in Mayberry know how to do well, it is cooking and canning.

Not long after Miss Addie and Coy Lee took over the operation of the business, a long overdue improvement was made to the store. A well was dug and running water piped into the store, so that indoor bathrooms could be installed. Of course, there were a few local diehards who claimed that they still preferred the little outhouse that sat behind the store, but the restrooms were an improvement much appreciated by 99% of the customers and all of the employees, especially in the winter. Not everyone who stops in from off the Parkway and visits the Trading Post has shopping as their main objective, but regardless of why they stop, most buy something before they leave.

When the indoor restrooms were added, a pair of unusual gender icons were placed on the restroom doors. These images were in keeping with the folksy Trading Post concept, and a lot of folks still notice that the icons bear a strong resemblance to Snuffy and Loweezy Smith, a couple of popular comic strip characters from a few generations ago. If you don't appreciate the significance of the images of Snuffy and Loweezy being associated with that store, then you might not be all that interested in the Mayberry Trading Post anyway.

During the years that the store was run by Miss Addie and Coy Lee, tourists would sometimes stop in and chat with the proprietors about "old country stores" they had visited in places like Jackson, Tennessee or Valle Crucis, North Carolina. Often, the visitors would conclude their chatting by comparing those stores with the Trading Post, sometimes going on and on about what one might find in those modernized ersatz old-time country stores, with the obvious implication being that maybe the proprietors of the Mayberry Trading Post should carry more of the stuff sold in those stores. Coy Lee would usually just nod and smile as they talked, and then go back to his whittling. He was happy with things just the way they were. He once said that for years he had been trying to find something that no one would buy – but he hadn't found it yet.

Sometime around 1990, it was discovered that the old steel gasoline tanks under the parking area were leaking into the ground. The new EPA regulations required that the Trading Post replace them or go out of the gasoline business. In any case, the old tanks would have to be removed. Miss Addie did the numbers and reached the conclusion that it would take many years of the profit from selling gasoline to cover the cost of installing new tanks, not to mention the expense of paying for the new pumps that would also be required to meet new EPA standards. So for the first time in over fifty years, it became no longer possible to buy gasoline at the Mayberry Store. No gas available at the Trading Post created something of an inconvenience for many local people, but most folks understood the decision.

For a number of years, Coy Lee Yeatts had been holding an annual fall event at the Trading Post that attracted crowds of people, both travelers from the Parkway and local folk. In the 1980's, Coy Lee was into the molasses business, which included growing and harvesting his own sorghum cane. After cutting the cane, he would run it through an ancient horse-powered sorghum press to extract the juice. Then the juice would be boiled down, a process requiring many hours of slow boiling and skimming, until the sorghum juice finally thickened into molasses. The entire manufacturing process was conducted right there beside the Mayberry Trading Post, and although growing sorghum, milling the cane, and making molasses in the traditional mountain fashion involved a tremendous amount of work, it also attracted droves of visitors to the store.

This demonstration of the almost obsolete skill of making "real" sorghum molasses was so popular that the Blue Ridge Parkway management talked Coy Lee into transferring the operation to Mabry Mill, four miles north on the Parkway. Coy Lee held the annual "molasses boiling" at the mill for several years, but as he got older and developed heart problems, he found that the reward to work ratio was just too small for him to continue. Although Coy Lee is no longer with us, the sorghum mill and molasses boiler he first set up at Mabry Mill are still used there to demonstrate, the vanishing skill of making molasses for the benefit of Parkway visitors,

During the same period of time that the molasses were being boiled, there were usually some other Mayberry folks working there beside the store, cooking up apples and stirring them down in a wood-fired copper kettle to make apple butter. This is a fall tradition that has continued for a very long time, with Gurney Royall and family making the apple butter at the Trading Post for the last several years.

Making apple butter is not quite as labor intensive as making sorghum molasses, but it still requires a lot of work. And just like the apple butter, the delicious homemade jams, jellies, and preserves made by Peggy Barkley, Pam Royall, and others from the Mayberry area, also require a lot of work. But if you try some of the homemade products that are available at the *Trading Post*, you will agree that they are all worth the effort.

The previous chapters of this little book contain several stories about local characters who frequented the Mayberry Store back when the other proprietors, mainly Cephas Scott and Coy Yeatts, were running it. But after the store was reincarnated as the Trading Post, I found that probably the most interesting people one would have encountered there were the proprietors themselves. It is unlikely that one would ever meet two more interesting and original people than either the late Miss Addie Wood or the late Coy Lee Yeatts.

Miss Addie

If you were ever in Mayberry and wanted to know where someone from the area used to live, or where their parents grew up, or where their great-grandparents came from, or who they married and how many kids they had, Miss Addie was the one to ask. She could also tell you where all the churches, mills, stills, and stores from a century past had been located. But one thing you needed to know – if you weren't from Mayberry, Bell Spur, or Meadows of Dan, then you would be considered a "tourist." No offense intended.

It used to be common wisdom over on Round Meadow Road that there was no one around, man or woman, who could outwork Addie Wood. She ran her own farm, milking several cows and selling the milk back when milking cows was done by hand. She also raised chickens and sold the eggs, and of course she cut the wood to heat her home, built fences, and cultivated the fields, just as any farmer had to do to run a successful farm operation. She must have felt like running a store was a vacation! If you are someone who thinks that hard work is bad for you, then you should know that when Addie Wood died in 2004, she had lived for 103 years. Just plain worked herself to death, someone said.

The use of the name Mayberry on the front of the Mayberry Trading Post is sometimes questioned by visitors who happen to stop in as they are traveling along the Blue Ridge Parkway. Occasionally, there is even the implied assumption that the Mayberry Trading Post is just another one of those businesses trying to capitalize on the fame of the Andy Griffith Show and the fictional television town of Mayberry. This is really not the case, and it is even likely that the name of the television Mayberry came from this place right here. Just to make it more official, it can also be shown that a dot noting the location of Mayberry appeared on maps of Virginia and in the Rand McNally Road Atlas for most of the first half of the twentieth century

In the years that Miss Addie Wood was operating the Mayberry Trading Post, she had her ready response for visitors who might ask her about a possible connection between the mountain Mayberry and the television Mayberry. She would begin her explanation by telling them, "Well, you know, Andy Griffith's mother was a nun...," and after a brief pause to enjoy the shocked look on the questioner's face, Miss Addie would continue. "Nunn was Andy's mother's last name. She was an N-u-n-n nun. Andy's mother was a Nunn who had relatives who lived up here on the mountain, near Mayberry. Andy would visit them sometimes when he was a boy." Information such as this makes a pretty strong circumstantial case for this place here being the source of the name of the television Mayberry, if not a documentable one.

Coy Lee:

Of all of the characters associated with the Mayberry Store over the past a century-and-a-half, few are more memorable than the co-proprietor of a few years ago, the late Coy Lee Yeatts himself.

For years, Coy Lee would talk to anyone who would listen about the great mineral riches he was convinced that lay beneath the ground somewhere around Mayberry. He read several books on geology and became surprisingly knowledgeable about certain aspects of the science. But the parts of the geology books where the science indicated that the ancient formations of the Blue Ridge Mountains in this area held little promise of valuable mineral deposits, he chose to ignore. His hope was likely to have been stimulated by the legend of a lost silver mine in the Mayberry area, somewhere near the Pinnacles of Dan. I am not a geologist, but some people who do know their geology have told me that they are confident that the tale of the lost Pinnacle silver mine is purely mythical.

As Coy Lee got older and his health became an issue, he spent more time inside the store, much of it sitting behind the counter and whittling. He specialized in making old-fashioned toy tops and carvings of wild animals, both of which he would sell in the store. He didn't make much money with his whittling, however, not that making money was his main objective. Whenever a child would come into the store and show an interest in his creation, Coy Lee would just give the child whatever he was working on. On at least one occasion, when an elementary school class on a field trip visited the Trading Post, Coy Lee gave every one of the kids (there were over twenty of them) an object that he had made.

It has been said that Coy Lee Yeatts was probably one person who never intentionally did a mean thing in his entire life. A little digging into his family history has shown this to be almost, but not quite, the case. The story of the exception is one worth telling.

One summer Sunday in 1927, a four-year-old Coy Lee was visiting at his grandmother's house when he came upon his Uncle Cardwell asleep in the front porch swing, his bare feet propped up on the porch railing.

Unfortunately for the uncle, little Coy Lee was a great fan of the Katzenjammer Kids, a popular Sunday newspaper comic strip of the day. The strip featured two young kids who were constantly playing pranks on their older relatives, and Coy Lee could not resist acting out on one of their naughty tricks he had seen in the funny papers just that morning. It obviously was a premeditated act, given that Coy Lee first went to the granary and obtained a short piece of fodder twine and then went into his grandma's kitchen and stole a big wooden match. Although he knew that he should never play with matches, Coy Lee slipped the piece of twine between his uncle's toes, then struck the match and lit the twine. The result was pretty much what one would expect. The uncle awoke with a bellow of pain, and after spotting Coy Lee grinning at him from behind an apple tree, chased him down and gave him a thorough paddling. Many years later, a less-than contrite Coy Lee admitted that, while this act was surely wrong, he might not be able to resist doing the same thing again if the opportunity ever arose.

It goes without saying that Mayberry, Virginia, is a low crime area. But back around 1990, however, a young and apparently inexperienced would-be-criminal walked into the store and over to the counter where Coy Lee sat, concentrating on his whittling. The would-be bandit then pulled out a small handgun and demanded all the cash on hand. Coy Lee reached under the counter like he was going to open the cash drawer, but instead of money, he pulled out his enormous old long-barreled Colt revolver. The would-be robber just turned and fled. Although the culprit was never identified, I think it's fair to say that both he and Coy Lee were very lucky that day.

Coy Lee Yeatts' health began declining around the year 2000, and he passed away in 2008. Throughout Coy Lee's long illness and for several years following his passing, his wife, Dale, was able to keep the store going. Finally, in 2012, when Dale's own health made her unable to operate the store, she turned it over to her younger cousin, Peggy Barkley. Here, at the beginning of 2014, Peggy continues as the Trading Post proprietor

It is worth noting that the little fertilizer and feed shed that was first built about 1930 to replace the old Bower store house has gone through many incarnations in the past eighty years. For the fifty years prior to the Mayberry Store becoming the Mayberry Trading Post, it did indeed serve as a storage facility for livestock feed, salt blocks, lime, fertilizer, and such. But in the 1940's, a section of the building was partitioned off to serve as a barber shop and later, that same section held a shoe repair and leather goods shop for several years.

In the years since the store became the Trading Post, the little building has housed an insurance agency, a rock shop, a real estate agency, and an antique store, sometimes two or more of the businesses at the same time. At this time, sad to say, there is no business located in the old building.

How much longer The Mayberry Trading Post will continue is anyone's guess, but there has been a store here at the intersection of these two country roads for over one hundred and fifty years now. The building itself still seems pretty sturdy, a testament to the owners having all kept a coat of paint on the sides and a sound roof on the top for all those years. The real question may be whether the store can remain a profitable business for many years longer, given that it is so dependent on tourism from the Blue Ridge Parkway. The Mayberry Store/Trading Post probably would have closed years ago, if it was not for the trade brought in by the Blue Ridge Parkway, and today there are those who are reluctant to support even the Parkway.

To me, the old store is a historical treasure. Just walking through and looking at its antiquated construction, with the tall windows, the patina on the time-worn counters, the add-on braces supporting the ceiling, and the long poplar board shelves along the walls, all of this creates a trip back in time and provides valuable lessons about how different life was in a rural community just a few generations ago. It is my hope that the Mayberry Store can capitalize on its historical momentum and continue to operate for many more years.

Regardless of its official name, it has always been *The Mayberry Store* to me. The store was almost fifty years old when I came into this world, and I like to think that it will continue for a long time after I am gone. This old store is a touchstone. When I come back to these mountains and leave the Parkway to drive into Mayberry, it is when I see the old store again that I begin to feel at home.

Special thanks to Peggy Barkley, Gary Barnard, Clifford Bowman, Margie Cartwright, Monroe Dalton, Sandra Dean, Larry Hutchins, Bernice Irvin, Jimmy Reynolds, Gerri Scardo, Alberta Sewell, Lawrence Sewell, Jeanette Shelor, Dale Yeatts, Fred Yeatts, Gerald Yeatts, and all of the current and former residents of Mayberry who took the time to share with me their memories of the Old Mayberry Store.

The Mayberry Store in 2012.

The Mayberry Trading Post is located just off the Blue Ridge Parkway, between mileposts 180 and 181, at the intersection of State Road 634 and Mayberry Church Road. The official mailing address is: Mayberry Trading Post, 883 Mayberry Church Road, Meadows of Dan, VA 24120.

jamcalex2@gmail.com.

29564072R00056

Made in the USA
Charleston, SC
17 May 2014